ADOPT-A DOG

CONTENTS

CHOOSING YOUR DOG

Many people choose a dog that they like the look of, without thinking too much about their lifestyle and how that dog might fit into it. A dog will hopefully be part of your family for 10-15 years. This is a big commitment and you'll need to make your choice wisely. These are a few things to bear in mind:

What are your energy levels?
A lot of dogs need three walks a day and some dogs need more intensive bursts of exercise too. Are you someone who likes to spend time outdoors even in the cold weather, or do you prefer curling up on a sofa with your dog snoring beside you?

Who's at home?
All dogs need companionship but some get very anxious when left alone for long periods of time, and this can result in barking and neighbours complaining. Do you have someone at home for more than half the day or are you all at work/school/activities from morning to night?

Where do you live?
If you live in a small apartment, it might not be practical to have a Great Dane taking up your living room. On the other hand, size isn't everything. Some big dogs, like St Bernards sleep for 16 hours a day, whilst Yorkshire Terrriers are tiny but super-charged. A big breed will need a lot of exercise, but if you live near a park, then apartment living won't necessarily be a problem.

Can you make time for grooming?
Some dogs need daily grooming and most dogs shed. Are there any people you are close to who are allergic? If this is a problem, you might want to go for a breed like a Poodle, which has tight curly fur that doesn't shed or trigger allergies.

Who will the dog be living with?
If you have babies or toddlers in your house, you'll need a dog that doesn't mind getting mauled around a bit. If you have cats or other pets, you'll need to have a tolerant dog with a low prey drive.

This book outlines the characteristics of some 35 dog breeds, but there are plenty of websites that will give you information about the hundreds of other options. Don't hesitate to talk to vets, breeders and trainers to get a full picture of what life with your dog might be like.

DOG GROUPS

The Kennel Club in the United Kingdom recognises seven breed groups of dogs. These groups organise the hundreds of purebreed dogs into categories with similar traits; terriers, hounds, gundogs, etc. Whilst there is often a lot of variation within each category, it can be helpful to bear in mind what group your breed belongs to, as it can make sense of some of their characteristics. Pastoral dogs, for instance, were bred to look after a herd of cattle. They will be smart, but protective and a bit nervous – always trying to guard their 'herd'. Working dogs often operated as part of a pack, therefore they will need a lot of companionship and don't like to be left alone.

The seven groups recognized by the UK Kennel Club are: Hound, Terrier, Working, Pastoral, Gundog, Utility and Toy. The American Kennel Club and other clubs around the world divide the groups up slightly differently, but along broadly similar lines.

GUNDOG GROUP

Dogs like pointers, retrievers, setters and spaniels were bred to help hunters identify, flush out or recover game. They are usually medium to large dogs; good-natured, playful and love to fetch. Very smart and athletic, they need plenty of exercise and companionship. They can make good family pets as they are loyal and obedient.

≈

Barbet   Irish Settler   Pointer

TERRIER GROUP

Terriers were bred to hunt small animals like rats. They are energetic, playful and independent. They need a lot of exercise and grooming and can be quite noisy and naughty. Their name comes from the word *terra* meaning 'earth' in Latin, and they love digging.

≈

Bull Terrier   Scottish Terrier   Border Terrier

HOUND GROUP

Hounds are the oldest type of hunting dog. There are two types of hound. Sighthounds are sleek and speedy – like the Greyhound, Whippet or Foxhound. Scenthounds, like the Bloodhound and the Beagle, are slower and more easygoing. Hounds are reliable dogs and good companions, but they can be stubborn, and sighthounds can sometimes be a bit jumpy.

≈

Basset Hound   Dachshund   Greyhound

PASTORAL GROUP

Dogs in this group were bred for farmwork. They are smart, obedient, independent and athletic. They need plenty of exercise and stimulation. They also often need lots of grooming, as they usually have a weatherproof double coat to protect them from the elements. Whilst they make wonderful, devoted pets, they can be very protective of their 'herd', and can sometimes bark or nip at strangers.

≈

Collie   German Shepard   Corgi

TOY GROUP

Toy dogs have a range of personalities and looks. In fact the only thing they have in common is that they were bred to be small. What they lack in stature, they often more than make up for in personality. Many of them descend from terriers and spaniels, and are quite feisty, whilst others have a more easygoing personality.

≈

Toy Poodle   Pug   Chihuahua

WORKING GROUP

Working dogs are big and strong, bred to perform tasks like pulling sleds or guarding property. They are usually intelligent and companionable. They need a lot of training so they don't become too protective, as well as a lot of exercise. Many working dogs have thick fur, which needs a lot of grooming.

≈

Boxer   Giant Schnauzer   St. Bernard

UTILITY GROUP

The only thing the dogs in this category have in common is that they don't fit into any of the other groups. Many of them were bred for a purpose that no longer exists. For example, a Dalmatian was bred to run alongside horse-drawn carriages. A Chow Chow was bred as a general purpose herding, pulling and guarding dog in Ancient China. Bulldogs used to work as fighting dogs, but when this was banned they had the aggression bred out of them, becoming companion dogs. There are, therefore, a broad variety of shapes, sizes and character traits in this group.

Bulldog   Dalmatian   French Bulldog

Boston Terrier   Chow Chow

PUREBREED DOGS

The advantage of choosing a purebreed dog is that it will have many predictable physical and character traits. You can be pretty sure that a Whippet will be energetic, a Collie will be smart and a Labrador will be loyal, as well as knowing exactly how they'll look and what they'll need in terms of grooming and exercise.

The downside of purebreed dogs is that often they were not bred to be pets, so you have to deal with behaviours that are better suited to hunting or herding and which can be a nuisance in daily life.

The other downside that there is a lot of inbreeding, which leads to health problems, and a purebreed's lifespan is much shorter than that of a mixed breed dog. This is especially true of dogs with flat faces like Pugs and Bulldogs.

When you buy a purebreed dog, make sure you get it from a responsible breeder. Because of the high value of purebreeds, there are a lot of irresponsible breeders who run 'puppy mills', keeping dogs in inhumane conditions. The puppies from these breeders can be stressed and have personality problems.

AFGHAN HOUND

≈

Size: Large
Good for apartment living: Yes
Grooming needs: High
Shedding: Medium
Exercise needs: High
Companionship needs: Medium

≈

≈

A tall, slim, elegant dog with a long, thick coat of fur designed
to keep it warm in the mountains of Afghanistan. It's a very
athletic breed – a fast runner and great jumper. Afghan Hounds
are generally relaxed indoors so can suit apartment living,
but they do need lots of exercise and attention, as they can
be stubborn and a bit stand-offish if their confidence is not
encouraged. Their silky coat requires a lot of grooming.

≈

BASSET HOUND

≈

Size: Medium
Good for apartment living: Yes
Grooming needs: Low
Shedding: Medium to high
Exercise needs: Medium
Companionship needs: High

≈

≈

One of the most dependably friendly breeds. They have
clownish looks with short legs, long, floppy ears and love-me-
eyes, but many people are surprised how bulky and sturdy they
are up close. Basset Hounds can be very lazy and need to be
exercised regularly or they will get fat, waddly and unhealthy.
This is a stubborn breed that's quite hard to train. They are
scenthounds, bred for hunting, and if they've picked up an
interesting smell, it's very hard to pull them away.

≈

BEAGLE

≈
Size: Medium
Good for apartment living: Yes
Grooming needs: Low
Shedding: Medium
Exercise needs: Medium
Companionship needs: High
≈

≈

The Beagle is a popular pet as it is quite small but has lots of big dog qualities. It is a gentle, playful and smart breed, but as with other hound dogs, it can be stubborn and hard to train. Beagles love to eat, and if their begging is indulged and/or they don't get enough exercise, they can become fat and unwell. When training a Beagle, don't use a food reward too often or they will only respond to you when you have a treat in your hand. Beagles are pack animals and need a lot of company or they can become distressed and destructive.

≈

BORDER COLLIE

≈
Size: Medium
Good for apartment living: No
Grooming needs: High
Shedding: Medium
Exercise needs: High
Companionship needs: High
≈

≈

The Border Collie is one of the most intelligent but challenging types of dog. It was bred to herd sheep, and it has a restless, darting energy, perfect for guarding a large flock, but not so great if it's kept in confined spaces. Border Collies need a huge amount of mental and physical stimulation – they can chase balls and sticks all day long – and if they don't get this, they can get hyperactive, barky and destructive. But with the proper training, this is a breed that will really reward.

≈

BORDER TERRIER

≈
Size: Small
Good for apartment living: Yes
Grooming needs: Medium
Shedding: Medium
Exercise needs: Medium
Companionship needs: High
≈

≈
A small dog with a big personality. Border Terriers have a face
that looks a bit like an otter's and a rough, wiry coat. They were
bred to help drive foxes out of their hiding places and they
have an inquisitive, friendly personality. They are less stubborn,
less barky and more adaptable than some of the other terriers.
This makes them well-suited to apartment living and they are a
popular family dog.
≈

BOSTON TERRIER

≈
Size: Small
Good for apartment living: Yes
Grooming needs: Low
Shedding: Low
Exercise needs: Low
Companionship needs: Medium
≈

≈
Descended from a cross between a Bulldog and a terrier, this
dog combines the gentlemanly charm of a Bulldog with the
playfulness of a terrier. They are loyal, eager to please and easy
to groom. They are not too barky, so good for apartment living.
On the downside, they do drool a lot and can have a lot of
health problems.
≈

BRUSSELS GRIFFON

≈
Size: Small
Good for apartment living: Yes
Grooming needs: Low
Shedding: Medium
Exercise needs: Low
Companionship needs: Medium
≈

≈
A toy dog with a big, clownish personality. He's a great climber and can get into tricky (and dangerous) situations. Very independent and curious and not very easy to train, the Brussels Griffon needs a firm hand, especially around housebreaking. He's a good watchdog and doesn't need much exercise.
≈

BULLDOG

Size: Medium
Good for apartment living: Yes
Grooming needs: Low
Shedding: Medium
Exercise needs: Low
Companionship needs: Medium

A sweet-tempered, low energy breed that doesn't need a lot of exercise or grooming. They are good family pets due to their placid, friendly nature. They are very snorty, snuffly and drooly and have lots of health problems. Their average lifespan is only seven years and vet bills tend to be high.

CHIHUAHUA

≈
Size: Small
Good for apartment living: Yes
Grooming needs: Low
Shedding: Low
Exercise needs: Low
Companionship needs: Medium
≈

≈
A very eccentric, funny little dog that can either be barky and
aggressive or friendly and placid. This has to do with both
genetics and training. If a Chihuahua comes from a neurotic
bloodline, there's not much you can do to make it relax.
However if you get a good Chihuahua and train it well, she can
be a fun, characterful addition to the family. They are very hard
to house train and they do not like cold weather, so you might
want to have an indoor litter box for this breed.
≈

CHOW CHOW

Size: Large
Good for apartment living: Yes
Grooming needs: High
Shedding: High
Exercise needs: Medium
Companionship needs: Medium

A beautiful, bear-like dog with a dignified but not very cuddly
personality. The Chow Chow doesn't need a huge amount
of exercise, and is usually quiet and peaceful in the home. Its
origins are as a guard dog in Ancient China, and without a
firm hand, it can become aggressive and overprotective of its
owners. Its long coat needs a lot of grooming and sheds a lot.

DALMATIAN

Size: Large
Good for apartment living: No
Grooming needs: Low
Shedding: High
Exercise needs: High
Companionship needs: High
≈

≈
Dalmatians have had a lot of inbreeding, so you must be
careful in selecting a Dalmatian from the right breeder. A good
Dalmatian is a polite gentleman of a dog; a loyal companion,
who enjoys plenty of exercise and play time. However, a badly
bred Dalmatian can be loud, neurotic and aggressive, as well as
suffering from lots of health issues. They're not well-suited to
apartment living and shed a lot of fur.

≈

DACHSHUND

≈

Size: Small or medium
Good for apartment living: Yes
Grooming needs: Low to high (depending on type)
Shedding: Medium
Exercise needs: Low
Companionship needs: Medium

≈

≈

A sparky 'sausage dog' with a great sense of humour. Its name
in German literally means 'badger dog'. It was bred to flush out
badgers and other underground dwellers from their burrows,
and as a result these dogs do like to dig! They come in larger
and smaller sizes and with different coats – long, wiry or short.
On the whole, long-haired Dachshunds are more mellow and
wire-haired ones are more aggressive. They are quite stubborn
and can be hard to train, but also make loyal, fun family pets.

≈

FRENCH BULLDOG

≈

Size: Medium
Good for apartment living: Yes
Grooming needs: Low
Shedding: Low to medium
Exercise needs: Low
Companionship needs: High

≈

≈

A fun-loving, easygoing dog who does equally well in the countryside or in an apartment. Young French Bulldogs are much more lively and playful than you might expect. Older dogs are more sedate. Frenchies, as they're known, don't need much exercise and are easy to groom. Health issues as well as drooling and flatulence are common, as with most flat-faced breeds. Be careful near water as Frenchies are terrible swimmers and can easily drown.

≈

GERMAN SHEPHERD

≈
Size: Large
Good for apartment living: Potentially
Grooming needs: Medium
Shedding: High
Exercise needs: High
Companionship needs: High
≈

≈
German Shepherds are smart, trainable dogs that have been
bred for lots of different purposes, and so their personalities
can vary enormously depending on their heritage. They can be
mild and mellow or vigorous and aggressive if they were bred
for protection. They need a lot of training but can be a fantastic
family companion dog if chosen from the right breeder.
≈

IRISH WOLFHOUND

≈
Size: Large
Good for apartment living: No
Grooming needs: High
Shedding: Medium
Exercise needs: High
Companionship needs: High
≈

≈
A gentle giant, the Irish Wolfhound is an easygoing but playful
breed that does well with plenty of space and companionship.
She needs a quite a lot of exercise and responds well to
patient training with plenty of rewards. She does need a lot of
grooming and also can be quite a flatulent breed.
≈

JACK RUSSELL

≈
Size: Small
Good for apartment living: Yes
Grooming needs: Low
Shedding: Medium
Exercise needs: High
Companionship needs: High
≈

≈

An energetic, bouncy-ball of a dog. This breed is great fun
and very rewarding, but you need to put the time in. They
can literally chase a ball all day long, and they need a lot of
companionship and stimulation. Bred to hunt rats, they are
enthusiastic chasers and diggers and do bark quite a lot. They
are very smart – the smartest of the terriers – and can be
trained to do pretty much anything.

≈

KING CHARLES SPANIEL

≈
Size: Small
Good for apartment living: Yes
Grooming needs: High
Shedding: Medium
Exercise needs: Low
Companionship needs: High
≈

≈
Also known as the English Toy Spaniel, this is a calm, comfort-loving breed, much happier cuddling on a sofa than running around the park. He needs a lot of companionship and attention and his long silky coat needs a lot of grooming. Great for apartment and city living.
≈

LABRADOR

≈
Size: Large
Good for apartment living: Potentially
Grooming needs: High
Shedding: Medium to high
Exercise needs: High
Companionship needs: High
≈

≈
One of the best dogs with children, the Labrador is a friendly,
easygoing family dog. Labradors need lots of exercise as they
can get fat and a bit jumpy if they've been indoors too much.
They respond well to training, but take a long time to mature
and have high energy when they are young. Because of their
intelligence and patience they are often used as guide dogs for
the blind and therapy dogs for people with autism.
≈

MALTESE

≈

Size: Small
Good for apartment living: Yes
Grooming needs: High
Shedding: Low
Exercise needs: Low
Companionship needs: High

≈

≈

A sweet, gentle breed with long, silky fur. They are quite playful
and like enclosed spaces – small yards and houses. They
can be quite barky, especially if they are left alone too often.
They are a non-shedding dog (good for people with allergies)
but they do need a lot of grooming. They can be hard to
housebreak and sometimes need an indoor litter tray.

≈

MEXICAN HAIRLESS

≈
Size: Small or medium
Good for apartment living: Yes
Grooming needs: Low
Shedding: Low
Exercise needs: Medium
Companionship needs: High
≈

≈
Also known as the Xoloitzcuintle (or the Xolo – prounounced show-low), this is a strange looking beast with a hairless body and a wrinkly face. If you can get beyond his looks, he's a good dog. He comes in small or large sizes and is mostly smart, obedient and friendly. He needs a lot of companionship, has a tendency to bark, and can be quite protective. Grooming of course is very easy!
≈

PEMBROKE WELSH CORGI

≈

Size: Medium
Good for apartment living: Yes
Grooming needs: Medium
Shedding: High
Exercise needs: Medium
Companionship needs: Medium

≈

≈

The Queen's own dog breed, the Corgi is a big dog on short legs. It was bred as a herding dog, and like all herding dogs, it is a bright, intelligent breed. Corgis makes great companions and watchdogs, only barking when necessary. They are easy to train, but like other herders, they like to chase smaller animals and are best kept on a lead. Corgis need quite a lot of grooming but only moderate amounts of exercise.

≈

POMERANIAN

≈

Size: Small
Good for apartment living: Yes
Grooming needs: High
Shedding: High
Exercise needs: Low
Companionship needs: High

≈

≈

A cocky, spirited, fluffball of a dog. Pomeranians are generally
friendly and playful, but can be aggressive to other dogs. They
are very territorial and tend to bark a lot, which should be
trained out of them when young. They shed a lot and need a
lot of grooming. Not a great choice of pet with young children,
as they don't like being roughly handled.

≈

POODLE

Size: Small, medium or large
Good for apartment living: Yes
Grooming needs: Low
Shedding: Very low
Exercise needs: High
Companionship needs: High

≈

≈

Poodles are smart and energetic dogs – easy to train and
protective, but not overly so. Their fur is tightly curly and
doesn't shed, so is great for allergy sufferers (although it does
need to be trimmed regularly). They need a lot of exercise and
can be anxious dogs if left alone too much. They can make a
great family pet.

≈

PUG

≈

Size: Small
Good for apartment living: Yes
Grooming needs: Low
Shedding: Low
Exercise needs: Low
Companionship needs: High

≈

≈

Sweet and steady, the Pug is a great companion. They usually
love children, and are sometimes called 'shadow' dogs, as they
will shadow you around wherever you go, always wanting to
be close to their owner. Pugs can be lazy and stubborn and can
easily get fat if they aren't forced to exercise regularly. As with
other flat-faced dogs, they often have breathing and
health problems.

≈

ROTTWEILER

≈
Size: Large
Good for apartment living: No
Grooming needs: Medium
Shedding: Medium
Exercise needs: High
Companionship needs: High
≈

≈
Descended from the herding dogs of the Ancient Romans,
the Rottweiler (or Rottie) is a strong-bodied, strong-minded
dog that can be very rewarding for the right owner. They are
known for their endurance, intelligence and strength, but they
also have territorial instincts that can lead to aggression. With a
confident owner, plenty of training and plenty of exercise they
will be placid, obedient, friendly and steadfast companions.
≈

SCHNAUZER

≈

Size: Small, medium or large
Good for apartment living: Yes
Grooming needs: Low
Shedding: Low
Exercise needs: High
Companionship needs: Medium

≈

≈

The name 'Schnauzer' comes from the German slang for
moustache, and the Schnauzer does indeed stand out for his
remarkable facial hair. They are lively, sensitive dogs; smart but
stubborn. They make good watchdogs as they are alert and
protective, but they need an owner who will show them who's
boss, so that they don't get too assertive.

≈

SCOTTISH TERRIER

≈
Size: Medium
Good for apartment living: Yes
Grooming needs: High
Shedding: Low
Exercise needs: Low
Companionship needs: Medium
≈

≈
The Scottie, as he is affectionately known, is a rugged little
dog that is playful, loyal and fiercely independent. He is a
fearless breed, happy to pick fights with dogs much bigger than
himself. He responds well to praise and treat-based training,
and much less well to rough handling. The Scottie needs
regular brushing and clipping, but doesn't shed much hair.
≈

SHIBA INU

≈
Size: Medium
Good for apartment living: No
Grooming needs: Medium
Shedding: Medium
Exercise needs: High
Companionship needs: Medium
≈

≈
A handsome, fox-like dog whose fiercely independent spirit
makes her quite a challenging companion. The Shiba Inu is an
extremely fast runner, and must be kept on a lead at all times.
She is often aggressive towards other dogs and loves to chase
cats and other small animals. She can also be destructive when
she doesn't get enough exercise. When she gets cross she lets
out a yelp that sounds like a scream.
≈

SIBERIAN HUSKY

≈

Size: Medium
Good for apartment living: No
Grooming needs: High
Shedding: Medium
Exercise needs: High
Companionship needs: Medium
≈

≈

A smart, playful, good-natured dog that was bred to work in
a pack, pulling sleds. Huskies are talented escape artists with
a high prey drive (they will chase cats or anything else that
moves). They need to be kept on a lead at all times with a high
fence around the yard. They are friendly with other dogs and
children, but need a lot of companionship and exercise or they
can become destructive.

≈

ST BERNARD

≈
Size: Very large
Good for apartment living: Potentially
Grooming needs: High
Shedding: High
Exercise needs: High
Companionship needs: Medium
≈

≈
A massive, calm, sensible dog that was bred to rescue lost travellers in the Swiss Alps. Although they do need lots of exercise due to their size, they are not a particularly energetic breed and enjoy a long walk in the snow, rather than endless games. They need a lot of companionship and are quite messy dogs, drooling and shedding a lot. Due to their heavy coat, they suffer in hot climates.
≈

STAFFORDSHIRE BULL TERRIER

≈

Size: Medium
Good for apartment living: Yes
Grooming needs: Low
Shedding: Medium
Exercise needs: Medium to high
Companionship needs: Medium to high

≈

≈

This tough little breed is fearless and loyal. Smart, stubborn
and athletic, Staffies respond well to training and can make
a fantastic family dog. Although they are generally calm, low
energy dogs, they were originally bred for fighting, and if not
properly trained and loved, they can be aggressive. They need
plenty of exercise and companionship and are easy to groom.

≈

WHIPPET

≈
Size: Medium
Good for apartment living: Yes
Grooming needs: Low
Shedding: Low
Exercise needs: Medium
Companionship needs: Medium
≈

≈

Closely related to the Greyhound, the Whippet was bred as
a sighthound to catch rabbits and small prey. Although they
don't need long walks, they need to be able to channel their
energy into short bursts of high speed activity. They can reach
35kmh in seconds flat! Adult Whippets are usually calm and
friendly dogs. They love climbing onto sofas and beds and
falling asleep in their owner's lap.

≈

YORKSHIRE TERRIER

≈
Size: Small
Good for apartment living: Yes
Grooming needs: High
Shedding: Low
Exercise needs: Low
Companionship needs: Medium
≈

≈
The Yorkie is a lively and inquisitive terrier, always trotting
around to see what's going on. He has a tendency to yap a
lot, which should be trained out of him at a young age. Despite
his long fur, he doesn't shed much, so is great for people
with allergies. It's a small breed, but within the breed, smaller
Yorkies tend to be more neurotic and larger Yorkies a bit more
chilled out.
≈

CROSSBREEDS

Crossbreeds are the result of mixing two or more different types of purebreed dogs. Also known as 'designer dogs', breeders aim to combine the best characteristics of each breed, as well as broadening the gene pool, and therefore hopefully eliminating some of the health problems of the purebreeds.

The downside of the crossbreed is that both their looks and personalities are hard to predict. Sometimes you get the worst traits of both breeds, and even in the same litter, two pups might turn out completely differently from one another.

Crossbreeds are often as expensive or more so than purebreeds, and the problems with irresponsible breeders are the same as with the purebreeds. Make sure you pick your pup from a trusted breeder who keeps both the mums and the pups in healthy conditions.

LABRADOODLE

≈

Size: Medium
Good for apartment living: Yes
Grooming needs: Low
Shedding: Low
Exercise needs: High
Companionship needs: High

≈

≈

A cross between a Labrador and a Poodle, this breed is often
smart like a Poodle, obedient like a Labrador and with curly fur
that doesn't smell or shed; good for allergy-sufferers. They are
usually friendly, energetic and good with children. Depending
on the type of Poodle, they can also be a more manageable
size than a Labrador.

≈

PUGGLE

≈

Size: Small
Good for apartment living: Yes
Grooming needs: Low
Shedding: Low
Exercise needs: Low
Companionship needs: High

≈

≈

A Pug mixed with a Beagle is also known as a Bug, a Buggle
or a Peagle. These dogs are friendly and loving like a Pug but
more active and inquisitive, like a Beagle. They don't need a lot
of exercise, but do need companionship. They usually have a
longer snout than a Pug, so have fewer breathing problems.

≈

COCKAPOO

≈
Size: Small to medium
Good for apartment living: Yes
Grooming needs: Medium
Shedding: Low
Exercise needs: Medium
Companionship needs: High
≈

≈
A cross between a Cocker Spaniel and a Poodle (usually a
Miniature or Toy Poodle). They are usually quite small, active
dogs with outgoing personalities like a Cocker Spaniel, and
tight, curly, low-shedding fur like a Poodle. However, they can
be anxious dogs and need a lot of companionship.
≈

GROOMING

Different dogs have different grooming needs, but all dogs need to be washed and brushed regularly. If you let your dog's fur get too matted, it can pull at the skin, making it sore. It will also result in a build-up of grease, which can lead to painful cysts. Grooming will keep them looking and feeling good, and will give you an opportunity to bond with your dog. It's also a great time to do an overall health check. While grooming, look for ticks and check the ears for unusual debris. Look at the eyes – some dog breeds get blocked tear ducts, resulting in staining. Sometimes water will flush out the irritant.

Make some time for grooming every day. Try to do this after exercise when your dog is tired and relaxed. Get pups used to grooming as early as possible. They'll soon learn to enjoy it!

BRUSHING

For long or medium dense coats, start with a slicker brush to get rid of tangles, and then follow with a bristle brush.

≈

For short, smooth coats, use a rubber brush followed by a bristle brush.

≈

If your dog has a rough, wiry coat, you may need to 'strip it'. this means using your hands to pull out the old fur, so that the new fur can grow in. Don't worry – this won't hurt your dog!

BATHTIME

Nobody likes a smelly dog, so make sure to wash your dog every one to three weeks, depending on how mucky he gets.

≈

Use a bath mat so that he doesn't slip around too much, and distract him with a dog toy if he's getting agitated.

≈

Wash the eyes and face with a plastic cup, as most dogs don't like to be sprayed directly.

≈

Make sure to use a special dog shampoo as dogs' skin can be very sensitive, and rinse it out thoroughly, as it can cause irritation if any is left in.

≈

NAIL TRIMMING

Long toenails can be painful for dogs, so keep nails trimmed regularly. The time to trim nails is after bathtime, when the nails are softened.

Start by separating out the toes, holding the paw gently.

≈

Using small, sharp clippers, clip at an angle, with your clippers almost parallel to the nail. Reward good behaviour with a treat!

COAT TRIM

If your dog enjoys a wash and a brush you might want to try trimming as the next step. This is usually done professionally, but if your dog is patient it doesn't take long to do it yourself.

Wash and brush your dog first, getting rid of all tangles.

≈

Make sure your clippers are nice and sharp, and choose clippers that are right for your dog's hair type.

≈

Push the clippers slowly in the direction of the hair growth, trying not to pull hair as you go.

≈

Make sure the blades on the clippers don't get too hot. Turn them off and check them regularly.

BRUSHING TEETH

Just like humans, dogs need to keep their teeth clean
so that they stay healthy. Vets recommend that you brush your
dog's teeth every day, but this can be easier said than done.
Once a week is usually enough, and if your dog gets agitated,
these are some tips:

Get your dog used to you touching her mouth by lifting her
lips and rubbing her gums with a moist cloth. If she lets you do
this without nipping you, give her a treat.

≈

Let her lick some doggy toothpaste off your finger so that
she gets used to the taste (never use human toothpaste;
the fluoride is very bad for dogs).

≈

After a few trials, try brushing her teeth very gently and reward
patience with a treat. There is no need to foam or rinse
after brushing.

FEEDING

Overweight or obese dogs are becoming
more common – when we lead busy lives
we sometimes stop exercising our dogs and
overfeed them to show them affection. Don't
let your dog get lazy and unhealthy. A fit, active
dog is a fun dog!

There is lots of conflicting advice about how
best to feed your dog. On the one hand,
commercial dog food is often made with very
low-grade meat and grain that is topped up
with a lot of preservatives and additives. On the
other hand, achieving a balanced, homemade
diet that suits your dog is very time consuming
and easy to get wrong. If you are using dog
food it is worth buying premium brands and
checking the list of ingredients.

Make sure to get the portion sizes right for your
dog. As your dog gets older they need fewer
calories, as they will be using less energy.

HEALTHY HABITS

Feed your dog twice a day. Try not to feed your dog directly before or after exercise.

≈

Throw away any stale food, and make sure your dog always has plenty of fresh water easily accessible.

≈

Never feed your dog from the table – this encourages bad behaviour like barking and begging.

TREATS

Treats should only be used for training. When you start, try to use something healthy, like slices of carrot. If your dog isn't interested, use the less healthy treats, but make sure to reduce the size of their main meal to take into account these extra calories. Remember – treats don't show your dog that you love them. Attention and games are much healthier ways to show your affection.

POISON FOOD

Some human food is fine for dog consumption but some things are really bad for a dog's health. These include: chocolate (especially dark chocolate), caffeine (keep used teabags away from curious dogs), grapes, currants, raisins, sultanas, nuts and salt.

TRAINING

Obedience training is an important part of being a responsible dog owner. Training won't solve all your problems – a jumpy, anxious dog can't be miraculously transformed – but it's a good place to start.

Dogs think and communicate in a very different way to humans, and training your dog will help them fit into a human world. Training also establishes a bond between dog and owner, based on respect. Finally, training gives your dog a mental workout, helping them feel useful and preventing boredom.

There are two main training methods – reward based training, in which good behaviour wins treats – and punishment based training, in which disobedience gets a yank on the chain or similar. Generally, it is reward based training that will lead to a well-adjusted, happy dog. However, using a sharp voice on occasion will also be part of teaching them respect and good manners.

TOP TIPS

Consistency: Make sure you use the same words every time. If you sometimes say "come" and sometimes "come here girl" it can be confusing.

≈

Start training as early as you can – at six to eight weeks if you're adopting a puppy.

≈

Keep training sessions short, and follow them with a fun activity or game.

≈

Only do training sessions when you're in a good mood. They should be fun and rewarding, not stressful.

≈

SIT

Hold a treat close to your dog's nose

≈

Move your hand up – his head will follow your hand and his bottom will lower.

≈

Once he's sitting down, say "sit" and give him the treat. Practice this five or six times a day, especially before walks and mealtimes.

STAY

Once your dog is an expert at 'sit', you can teach him to
stay in that position, although this is a harder command –
especially for puppies.

≈

Say "sit". Once he is sitting, open your palm in front of you
and say "stay". Then take a few steps back, rewarding him if he
stays, even for a few seconds.

≈

Gradually increase the number of steps back you take
before giving him the treat.

COME

This is an important command to teach dogs who have
a tendency to bolt as soon as they're let off the lead.

≈

Put a lead and collar on your dog and sit as far away from
him as the lead will allow.

≈

Say "come" and tug on the lead so he comes to you.
When he gets to you give him a treat and a cuddle.

≈

Now try without the lead, but keep practising in an enclosed
area until he's got the hang of it.

LEAVE IT

This command can be very important for dogs who like to chew things that might be harmful.

Hold a treat between your thumb and forefinger. When your dog tries to grab it, close it inside your fist and turn your palm down, saying "leave it".

≈

She will probably keep nosing your hand or start barking or even nipping you. Ignore this behaviour. As soon as her attention moves away from your hand and she looks at your face, say "good" and open your palm.

≈

Once you've done this a few times, move to the floor. Lie down and cover the treat with your palm. When she looks at your hand or tries to move it, say "leave it". When her attention breaks away, reward and praise her.

≈

Now try this again, but only covering the treat with your finger. If she tries to grab it, cover it with your palm again.

≈

Next, hold your dog on a lead in your left hand, and casually drop the treat with your right hand. When she tries to get it, say "leave it" and hold her back. When she stops pulling at the lead, give her the treat.

≈

Finally, try the exact same exercise but without the lead.

EXERCISE

How much exercise your dog needs depends
on her breed and age. Young dogs need a lot
of exercise to channel their energy so they
don't destructive. Adult dogs need to be kept
trim and fit so they don't get sick.

DAILY EXERCISE

Most dogs need around an hour of exercise a day. Usually this takes the form of two walks. Try to vary the walks to keep it interesting for you and your pup.

≈

If you have an active breed, like a terrier, they also need 30 minutes of hard exercise – running off the lead if possible and playing fetch.

OTHER EXERCISE IDEAS

Dog parks are a good place if your dog gets on with other dogs. If they're aggressive with other dogs, steer clear!

≈

Frisbee – make sure you have a dog-friendly Frisbee with soft edges.

≈

Rollerblade or bike ride – if you have a park or a low-traffic area where it's safe to do this, let your dog run alongside you. It's a great way to tire him out!

≈

Swimming – if you have a hound or a retriever who loves to swim, take your game of fetch to a pond. They'll love it.

Squeak!

WEATHER CONDITIONS

In extremely hot or cold weather it's best to keep outdoor exercise to a minimum. Try running up and down the stairs with your dog, or for smaller breeds, build an indoor obstacle course with cushions.

Published by Cicada Books Limited

Written by Tim Baker
Illustrated by Holly Maguire
Design by April

British Library Cataloguing-in-Publication Data.

A CIP record for this book is available from
the British Library.
ISBN: 978-1-908714-35-0

Printed in China

CO

Cicada Books Limited
48 Burghley Road
London NW5 1UE
T   +44 7890 431037
E   ziggy@cicadabooks.co.uk
W www.cicadabooks.co.uk